BOOKWORMS

Riding to the Rescue!

Police Cars

B.J. Best

Cavendish Square
New York

Published in 2018 by Cavendish Square Publishing, LLC
243 5th Avenue, Suite 136, New York, NY 10016

First Edition

Website: cavendishsq.com

CPSIA Compliance Information: Batch #CS17CSQ

Library of Congress Cataloging-in-Publication Data
Names: Best, B.J.
Title: Police cars / B.J. Best.
Description: New York : Cavendish Square Publishing, 2018. | Series: Riding to the rescue!| Includes index.
Identifiers: ISBN 9781502625731 (pbk.) | ISBN 9781502625670 (library bound) | ISBN 9781502625557 (6 pack) | ISBN 9781502625618 (ebook)
Subjects: LCSH: Police vehicles--Juvenile literature.
Classification: LCC HV7936.V4 B47 2018 | DDC 363.2'32--dc23

The photographs in this book are used by permission and through the courtesy of:

Cover Bruce Leighty/Photolibrary/Getty Images; p. 5 Studiodr/iStock/Thinkstock.com; p. 7 H. Mark Weidman Photography/Alamy Stock Photo; p. 9 Stanislav Halcin/Alamy Stock Photo; p. 11 Washington Stock Photo/Alamy Stock Photo; p. 13 Mel Longhurst/Corbis Documentary/Getty Images; p. 15 Ford Motor Company; p. 17, 21 Kali9/iStockphoto.com; p. 19 Yuri Acurs/E+/Getty Images.

Printed in the United States of America

Contents

There has been a car crash!

Someone might be hurt.

It is time to call the police!

Here comes a police car!

It has red and blue lights.

It has a loud siren.

KSPD
03-24

Other cars move out of the way.

A police car drives fast!

POLICE
NYPD

The police car arrives at the crash.

The police officers will help people who are hurt.

They will let other cars drive by safely.

POLICE
1902
TAXI
POLICE

A police car is the same shape as a normal car.

But it isn't built the same.

STATE TROOPER
NEW YORK
STATE POLICE
F.D. N.Y.
579

A police car is built to be strong.

It has a big **engine**.

It has a strong **frame**.

A police car has
a computer.

It has a radio so police officers can talk to each other.

It has a video camera.

POLICE
DEPT.

Police officers also
solve crimes.

They drive their cars to
crime **scenes**.

They ask questions.

They try to catch **criminals**.

POLICE
POLICE LINE DO NOT CROSS
POLICE
POLICE

Police officers help people.

They make sure people follow the law.

Their cars help them do their jobs!

New Words

criminals (KRIH-muh-nulz) People who break the law.

engine (EN-jin) Motor that powers a car.

frame (FRAIM) A car's body.

scenes (SEENZ) Places.

Index

About the Author

B.J. Best lives in Wisconsin with his wife and son. He has written several other books for children. He has been helped by a police officer at a car crash.

About BOOKWORMS

Bookworms help independent readers gain reading confidence through high-frequency words, simple sentences, and strong picture/text support. Each book explores a concept that helps children relate what they read to the world they live in.